W9-AGC-573

HEY, MARFA

Also by Jeffrey Yang

Poetry

Vanishing-Line
An Aquarium

Translations

City Gate, Open Up by Bei Dao
Uyghurland, the Farthest Exile by Ahmatjan Osman (with the author)
June Fourth Elegies by Liu Xiaobo
East Slope by Su Shi

Edited Volumes

The Sea Is a Continual Miracle: Poems and Writings on the Sea by Walt Whitman
Time of Grief: Mourning Poems
Birds, Beasts, and Seas: Nature Poems from New Directions
Two Lines: Some Kind of Beautiful Signal (with Natasha Wimmer)

HEY, MARFA

Jeffrey Yang

Paintings and drawings by Rackstraw Downes

DISCARDED
from   Library

IOWA CITY
JAN -- 2019
PUBLIC LIBRARY

Graywolf Press

Copyright © 2018 by Jeffrey Yang

This publication is made possible, in part, by the voters of Minnesota through a Minnesota State Arts Board Operating Support grant, thanks to a legislative appropriation from the arts and cultural heritage fund, and a grant from the Wells Fargo Foundation. Significant support has also been provided by Target, the McKnight Foundation, the Amazon Literary Partnership, and other generous contributions from foundations, corporations, and individuals. To these organizations and individuals we offer our heartfelt thanks.

Special funding for this title was provided by the Lannan Foundation.

Thanks to the editors of the following publications in which some of these poems first appeared: *Almost Island* (India), *Der Grief* (Germany), the *New York Review of Books*, *Poetry*, *Poem-a-Day*, *Reliquiae Supplement 2017* (Cumbria: Corbel Stone Press), *Seedings* (Duration Press), and the anthology *Happiness, The Delight-Tree: An Anthology of Contemporary International Poetry*, edited by Bhikshuni Weisbrot, Darrel Alejandro Holnes, and Elizabeth Lara (United Nations SRS Society of Writers, 2017). "Seashell for C. D." is included in a forthcoming trilingual anthology of poetry edited by Dong Li in memory of C. D. Wright. "The Grass" was set to music by the composer Charo Calvo during a residency at the Studio for Electroacoustic Music at the Akademie der Künste and premiered at the Villa Elisabeth in Berlin in July 2018.

Published by Graywolf Press
250 Third Avenue North, Suite 600
Minneapolis, Minnesota 55401

All rights reserved.

www.graywolfpress.org

Published in the United States of America

ISBN 978-1-55597-819-8

2 4 6 8 9 7 5 3 1
First Graywolf Printing, 2018

Library of Congress Control Number: 2018934487

Cover design: Jeenee Lee Design

Front cover art: Rackstraw Downes, *Untitled*, no date. 6¼ x 9½ inches. Graphite on paper.
Back cover art: Rackstraw Downes, *Untitled*, no date. 6¼ x 9½ inches. Graphite on paper.

to the Lannan Foundation
for taking me there

to M., A., and Q.
for letting me stay

to T. and C.
for being there

to R. D.
for picturing the scale

to J. S., F. M., K. D.
for their devotion and care

and others near
here or there

for love

HEY, MARFA

信言不美
美言不信
　　　—老子 (中國春秋時代)

Truthful words are not beautiful
Beautiful words are not truthful
　　　　　—Old Master (Spring and Autumn Period)

. . . these lines curve through the desert

Hey, beautiful
Marfa . . .

Arrived at El Paso airport
hours away, first-time resident
for a month to stay

D. picked me up
drove the Prius beneath
an enormous bronze stallion
reared-up high with general astride
missing its priapus

Juárez

a stone's throw from El Paso

twin cities divided
across the highway
river
bridge
between the promise
of heaven and hell

Feminicidio
the tenth circle beneath the ice

From this side of la frontera

mirage of shimmering metal and glass
of another country, where

John and Alice exchanged vows

to his last live recording:
Olatunji "Ogunde"

In the Book of Last Words
Clara Schumann says, "You two
must go to a beautiful place this summer."

■

Aerostat balloon with radar/
camera, watching the border, watching
for, watching for . . .
Single eye
floating in the sky tied
by a line of
technology, in defense
of these states

■

Vast, flat desert
scrub, barbed wire
highway cuts through
tame wilderness

Water-pumping windmill
spins like a flying machine
abandoned to time

1 pecan farm
1 gas station
1 drive-in theater
Valentine, population 131
along the way to Marfa

Juárez

Playboy (2003): "And hell?"

R. B.: "Like Ciudad Juárez, our
curse and our mirror, the unquiet
mirror of our frustrations and of our vile
interpretation of freedom and our desires."

Journalist (2013): "If Juárez really were hell,
everybody in the city would be dead by now."

Miroslava Breach Velducea (1962–2017),
shot eight times at home in her car
taking her son to school
Thursday, March 23
A note left on her dead body:
"Por lengüona. Ahora sigue tu gobernador. El 80"

■

I don't know
which to hate more:
violence, or the causes of violence;
my hate, or the hate of others

In the Book of Last Words
Founding Father Benjamin Rush says,
"Be indulgent to the poor."

■

Rolling *adagio* into town
down San Antonio Street
a flash of home
long ago—*Escondido*
through the windshield
sand-lit adobe, arid heat, hidden signals

Ms. Mitchell recalls arriving as a bride
in 1894, and thought *she had reached the end of the world*

O. W. Williams, surveyor in 1901:
"Arrived in a windstorm—Marfa
is an exceedingly dusty town, and a
windstorm raises a tornado of dust."

The archaeologist Charles Peabody in 1909:
"The bare mountains take on the most
wonderful colors in the world, like that in
California, Spain, and Greece . . . ."

■

"Afar, the eye rests on nothing but gloomy mountains
of the most irregular and varied forms, while near,
a high, thick, thorny chaparral obstructs the road
and the view, as if guarding a paradise . . . ."
(Julius Fröbel, 1853)

All the names of the plants
All the names of the trees
All the names of the rocks

circle the rose-soft mountains

swallowed by sky
          by sand
                    by brush

in shade and shades of light

Juárez

The poorest district
of the state, tagged

on a wall
of the Heroic City:

LA POESIA
    SE VOLÓ
       LA
      BARDA
        ARMINE

In the Book of Last Words
William Blake says, "My beloved,
they are not mine—no—they are not mine."

In the Book of Last Words
Ignacio Cuevas says before his execution,
"I'm going to a beautiful place."

■

Ruperta Gongora

                        curandero healer,
born in Ojinaga in 1850, recalled
Marfa as a courthouse, jail, and depot

She watched Villa's occupation of Juárez
from El Paso, heard the music mingling with gunfire,
saw the dead bodies along the river banks

Her husband was killed by a horse

She mourned the capture of Mescalero
Apache Chief Alsarte by Mexican soldiers

Gongora died in 1960

She's buried at La Cementerio de la Merced,
where San Antonio Street crosses Austin

1937, Robert Reed Ellison recalled
Marfa around 1883: a depot, a section, and two tents:
"Joe Buhl, a Frenchman, had a saloon in one tent, and off a little ways a Chinaman
had a restaurant. No one was there except a Railroad agent and operator and two
section crews, all Chinamen."

L. C. Brite, cattleman, churchman, 1885:
"Before me was a new and untried country . . .
an experiment."

In the Book of Last Words
King Kalākaua says through *the machine that talks*,
"Tell my people I tried to restore our gods, our way of life."

The New Era, July 1, 1893:
"Marfa has 2 hotels, 1 railroad, 1 saloon, 2 churches, 1 fruit stand, 1 livery stable, 1 barber shop, 1 meat market, 2 lumber yards, a $95,000 Courthouse and Jail, Ladies Aid Society, 1 job printing office, 1 boot and shoe shop, 1 weekly newspaper, 2 blacksmithing places, 2 wood-working shops, 1 harness and saddle factory, stock yards and shipping pens, 4 dry goods and grocery stores, a small but well-ordered graveyard, a ministering children's league, over 60 pupils enrolled in public school, good wagon roads leading out in every direction, good society, liberal, progressive, intelligent people, a fine system of water works with over two miles of mains . . . "

■

Donald Judd, circa 1972:
"I kept the building but moved to West Texas with my two children, where I rented a small house on the edge of town. The house was quartered into eleven by eleven foot rooms. There was no furniture and none to be bought, either old, since the town had not shrunk or changed much since its beginning in 1883, or new, since the few stores sold only fake antiques or tubular kitchen furniture with plastic surfaces printed with inane geometric patterns and flowers."

■

Journalist Sterry Butcher, August 2007:
"I moved to Marfa from Austin in 1993. At the time, Marfa had two gas stations, two restaurants, two bars, one grocery store, a post office, two cops, and an art museum. And I thought, 'Wow, there's everything you need here and nothing more. There's no excess at all.'"

Substation

Gray day faraway water-tower potentiometer

enclosed by a series of right-angle triangles, guy-
line hypotenuse cables lengthening to anchor

pole, Johnny ball insulators down to cadmium
yellow reflectors, ten thousand faces reflected

in the eyes, finely tuned, harmonized, freight
train peeks by the horizon on the other side

A small town thrives in the desert, periwinkle
rose flesh tint homes mute ochre, brown earth

fenced substrate groomed weedlessness, dried
brush outside the perimeter, off-center lines

in semaphore crisscross the sky, as if ordinary
heralds of the light, as if Sassanian wings

above an Aspahan arch whisper weight-
lessly, "Your golden age has yet to come . . ."

X.

Et in Ataraxia ego
in a death-row state

And Liu Xiaobo in a cell
sentenced by nation-state

having chosen his fate long
ago, determined by the state

the state *which denies the word*
he has shown compassion for

each successive wave after wave
on which a wooden plank floats

Such compassion will ever be, O Osip,
the poet's social obligation and heroic feat

X.

Glass-study loci, wild

turkeys forage through
tended prairie grass

Redbreast across the way
alfresco with Dionysus

Time given space

to translate each line
of his mourning 4ths

X. wrote in darklight
across two decades

annual offerings to the dead
souls of June, unforgotten

fourth, time drops anchor
a needle pierces the heart

and the shadows, O Osip,
pay ten heavens for this earth

Reading

At the anti-penal colony
time served for four wandering
the circular corridors, I found

myself before the last door,
the forbidden one, the one
forever shut, key in my hand,

the agony burning inside me,
effortlessly it turned, and the light
glanced off the infinite cymbals

through the widening crack
of the threshold, onto my finger,
which froze into gold, and I fled

to the woods, fed on roots and berries,
hair grew long with the shadows'
voices, my silence a stolen tongue

Bob

Your lungs
     failed here
but not your heart, *For*
Love, carries on

    ■

Napped in the light of unknowing

Strange ring disrupted a dream

Clocks off, time lost, I awoke
to canary song

Among the settlers
watching the green star burn
the light-signal flashing over and over
steady drone of a dial tone

Winter-Spring 2011

Town's asleep today, as it was
yesterday, closed up, people

gone inside or elsewhere here
to nowhere, working, hiding, siesta

time. Freight train passes by, car
after car romance, outside the ice

factory relic, buzz of electricity, no station
stop, Cowboy Church but no drugstore

Poetry

Yoruba àshe: *make it happen*
                    in the pattern   of lightning
                        Eshu's gift   at
                            the crossroads
            Ram's horn   earth-
worm's breathless   plunge
            through the layers   ventilating
                horizons

.

In the Book of Last Words
Vicente Blasco Ibáñez says,
"¡Mi jardín … mi jardín!"

Conquistadors

Sunrise over a dirt road
by a low-wire fence, birdsong,
a rooster crows, then distant church bells
pealing arpeggios in the thin air

Two horses graze next to a roofless ruin

Light slowly swells, expands, fills
the heavens, awakens the undergrowth

and the blood of the defeated
running fast through the earth

■

Called "minorities by conquest"
swept along, on and beyond the state's
three reservations, land once
a republic "of raids and counterraids,
of alliances kept and broken"
of Patarabueyes, Jumanos, Sumas, Caddos
of Arbados, Cuthalchuces, Jicarillas, Lipans
of Cibolos, Kickapoos, Susolas, Quitoles, Malicones
of Neches, Coayas, Coyoteros, Atayos, Apaches, Comanches, Atakapans
of Piros, Mescaleros, Wichitas, Taovayas, Tonkawas
Bidais, Tejas, Cheyennes, Kiowas, Karankawas, Yutas
and on diverse nations known
through pages named
each stretch of sand, unspoken presence

Tyrrel Smith, born 1891:
"From the time we could ride we went on roundups.
It was back when there were few fences ...
Seems my best memories are of those experiences."

■

Metal billets   rolled into rods
pulled   through the dies
twisted barbs   unspooled
holding pens   by 1890 stock-
men's trade fixed   rangelands
fenced property   the far-off
sound   of a train whistle
as if   in a Mahler symphony
white steam   pouring through
"The Indian Barrier   Must Be
Removed"   and other stories

Winter count

on the Plains
painted on buffalo hide
    each image
a year's happening,
snowfall to snow-
    fall meteor
shower, witnessed
by the tribe
    chosen in common
experience, spiral
calendar history
    discontinuous
meanings of the symbols
living memory
    retold
through the seasons'
icons into stories

In the Book of Last Words
Founding Father Thomas Jefferson says,
"Is it the Fourth?"

.

In the Book of Last Words
Leonel Torres Herrera says before his execution,
"I am an innocent man and something very wrong is taking place tonight."

.

In the Book of Last Words
Frederick Douglass says, "Why,
what does this mean?"

Marfa Apocrypha

When they came to the crossing that night, Eliseo sent his two wives, two maids, and eleven children over the Río Bravo, and sent over that he had. Tarrying himself alone, back in the canyon, he danced under the moonlight until a stranger appeared, who wrestled with him through the night until the break of day. The stranger, seeing that he could not prevail against Eliseo, touched the hollow of Eliseo's thigh, which became loosened, but still Eliseo did not relent nor did he falter. And the stranger said, "Let me go, for the morning dawns." Who answered him, "So what it's morning? The day's as short as my journey's long. I won't release you unless you bless me." Then the stranger said unto him, "What is thy name?" And he said, "Eliseo." To which the stranger replied, "Thy name shall be called Eliseo no more, but Mar-phah: for you wrestle like a Russian powerhouse and dance like a bitter Lady." Then Eliseo demanded, "Tell me, I pray thee, thy name whom has the chutzpah to spy upon me and name me." Said he, "Wherefore now doest thou ask my name? I am no more than a stranger." And the stranger blessed him there, and rode away on his donkey toward the presidio. So Eliseo called the place Peguis, saying, "I have seen the Stranger face to face, and I was nearly destroyed, like a little chip of wood in the flame." Therefore, the children of Marfa eat not of the sinew that shrank in the hollow of the thigh, unto this day, because the stranger touched the sinew that shrank in the hollow of Eliseo's thigh.

The Lights

Drive out to the viewing site
no guarantee to see the Lights

Same sight as everywhere else
round the pavement, but there

you can relieve yourself inside

■

Echo City

November 17, 1871, Margaretha Schafer,
age twenty-one, writes in her 4 x 3" diary
translated from the German by her granddaughter:
"In Echo City
we had an imposing view of the mountains. The beautifully
high mountains with their shapes looking as if alive.
Shortly before 3 we passed the Devil's gate. It lasted 20 minutes!
On the 17th in the morning we lost one of our passengers.
He was a funny chap. He went outside for a breath of fresh air.
The train left and he had to stay behind. Everybody was sorry.
In the afternoon we visited a China Hut.
The people were friendly and clean."

Most of the residents'
first tongue is Spanish

Others have come and gone
over the years

like those found sealed in a freight car
of copper ore, dying of thirst,
jailed, then deported with thirty more

back East, 1908

Cave

Celadon fragments, hearth features, in situ
stoneware, hammered gold image of Shou
Xing, god of longevity, bones, sherds, coins

left in the camps, yet not one written scrap
no note no letter no list no diary, a name
scratched on a cliff-face, of those disappeared

building the lines West, blasting tunnels, carving
roadbeds out of mountains, *jup seen you* ritual,
search the Sierra for the remains of lost friends

One Wong Hau-hon worked on the Canadian Pacific,
reminisced forty-four years later, H. M. Lai translates:

I first came to Canada in 1882 on a sailing vessel. . . . After our arrival at Yale, we had only worked two days when the white foreman ordered the gang to which I was assigned to move to North Bend. . . . Some died as they rested beneath the trees or laid on the ground. When I saw this I felt miserable and sad. . . .

When we were passing China Bar on the way, many of the Chinese died from an epidemic. As there were no coffins to bury the dead, the bodies were stuffed into rock crevices or beneath the trees to await their arrival. Those whose burials could not wait, were buried on the spot in boxes made of crude thin planks hastily fastened together. There were even some who were buried in the ground wrapped only in blankets or grass mats. New graves dotted the landscape and the sight sent chills up and down my spine. . . .

Twenty charges were placed and ignited but only eighteen blasts went off. However, the white foreman, thinking that all of the dynamite had gone off, ordered the Chinese workers to enter the cave to resume work. Just at that moment the remaining two charges suddenly exploded, Chinese bodies flew from the cave as if shot from a cannon. Blood and flesh were mixed in a horrible mess. . . .

Later I moved again and worked in a barren wilderness for more than a year. There more than 1,000 Chinese laborers perished from epidemics. In all, more than 3,000 Chinese died during the building of the railroad from diseases and accidents. . . .

I am now 62 and I have experienced many hardships and difficulties in my life. . . . Yet now the government is enforcing 43 discriminatory immigration regulations against us. The Canadian people surely must have short memories!

琮*

Alive   in the fragments
heaven-shattered   shards
of stone   divine   particles
gleaned   in the half-light
perquisite of the gods   bestowed
in the shadow of the signs   by
the gravity   of the center-
seated spirit   humanity encodes
for the given sequence   a
simplicity of form   channeled
energy entombed   for
millennia   now un-
buried   useless
absolute   in the actual
object   function lost   to time
and circumstance   civilization
long gone   its power   lost
its aura   unfading   gently
tapers   down   the carved
symmetry   corner
bars   theriomorphic mask
heaven   embedded in earth
ladder   bracelet   or
marked   ancestral heraldry
found   around the dead
body   placed   in a circle
the relevant   passage

---

* *cong* (or *tsóng*): Neolithic ritual vessel made of stone, often jade, carved as an elongated square block that encloses a hollow, cylindrical tube. Its original use possibly astronomical.

Circle

vultures mark the sky
at sunset, divine artifice
carrying the dead from here
to clearer air, thermal up-
drafts under unmoving
wings, as if held by invisible
strings, gentle gyre, way-
ward winds in which
vultures mark the sky

Cave

Carbon handprint in a cave

beside a ferrous oxide antelope

Figure approaching a gate
to sun, one standing astride

flowering star, swallow nests of mud
above: barnacles on the cliff-face

Substation

Live lines lead

to the substation grid
vital node

between the tracks and a lonely
row of small houses

where an asphalt road
meets lattice towers, high-

tension buses and switches

transmission lines sail to lightning
gyres, lugs fix cross strut to

strut transformers induct, step

up step down, fenced-off
structure, wooden pylons

          against sand and sky

insulators, isolators, arresters
X'd constructed monument

to the unknown

prisoner, receding cube within
cube of walls of air, pantographic

          galvanized gantry
breaker and fuse, relay equipage

Kilovolts hum unending
                        ommmmm
of the lamp's transmission
down at the switchyard

Through the body
electromagnetic

         lines bond totemic, linked
desert succulence less
wilderness, less relent
less waste
land
                  lines'
further prospect

toward a purer array of sun

In the Book of Last Words
Ava Gardner says, "I'm so tired."

∎

Travel Writing

This place Hollywood
likes to masticate for a bit
to spit out its landscape

Tourists come to look
at the edge of the dirt
where artists play and work

Some call it *el hogar*, some home
for roughly two thousand souls

by chance, the same number of Hupas
left at the place where the trails return

Some stay along the way to somewhere
else planned or unknown, but if you go

to Jamaica, you must try the grass called
khus khus,* its *sweet scent from its roots*, Zora
Neale tells us, *the very odor of seduction*

---

* Not to be confused with the scented grass called *kuśâ* the Buddhist monk-translator Xuanzang mentions on
  his visit to the city of Kiu-she-kie-la-po-lo, the center of the kingdom of Magadha, in Huili's biography, the
  same grass which Krishna tells Arjuna to make a meditation seat out of in the Gita.

Colonel Ellison, 1937:
"And a little while after night came,
a full moon rose up over the mountains
and it was still a beautiful sight to see
those mountains by moonlight. They looked
like they had just moved up a little closer."

■

Moon full above the old tracks
weaving back on foot from Padres
making way, long past midnight
and the dark houses uphill
to blindness, wind
at the lips, already a memory
Dew gathers on the yucca leaves
Shadows guide the way toward
the door of forgetting, opening
out to the next day's suffering

Reading

Chestnut trees bloom in Vienna
as the sea loves a pebble on its sands

At night, in the coffeehouse, by the
iridescent flicker of the carbide lamp

drinking the letters from K. to M.
through a peephole, they bleed, hers

burned to ash, half a life's romance left
for the public, history's convention of

ghosts who *devour the true word*
across the boundary, to this elevation

Flames of golden leaves in a dream:
"I am you and you are me, on and on

you transmutate into me, I merge into
you, you catch fire, I take an old coat

and beat you with it, but the transmutation
begins again, until you are no longer there

and I am on fire, I beat the fire with the coat
to no avail, the fear that such things cannot

extinguish fire, then the fire brigade arrives
and you are saved, though changed, now

spectral, as if drawn with chalk against
the dark, you fell, lifeless, or maybe fainted

with joy at having been saved, into my arms,
or maybe it was I who fell into someone's arms"

In the Book of Last Words
Ricky Lynn Lewis says before his execution,
"Let me rest. It's burning."

■

Cave

The cave de Sahagún recorded
as unearthed in *Technicians of the Sacred*

becomes long and deep; it widens, extends,
narrows. It is a constricted place, a narrowed place,
one of the hollowed out places. There are roughened places;
there are asperous places. It is frightening, a fearful place,
a place of death. It is called a place of death because there is dying.
It is a place of darkness; it darkens; it stands ever dark.
It stands wide-mouthed; it is wide-mouthed; it is narrow-mouthed.
It has mouths which pass through.
I place myself in the cave. I enter the cave.

Cave

A place once known as Despoblado
to wayfarers—desolate, uninhabitable
wilderness outside the settlements

Pueblos at La Junta de los Rios

River valley once green and fertile

until one day the devil appeared
on a string stretched out from the Chinati
Mountains south to Sierra de la Cruz

The devil laughed and danced on the line
across the valley, breathing fire down
on the farmlands, destroying the fields

But then a priest lured the devil away
and drove him into a cave
and the people sealed it with rock and fire
and a cross on Santa Cruz Mountain

Devil

They told us a story about the devil,
mala cosa, small in stature with a beard
whose face they could never see clearly
who traveled from house to house
with a flaming piece of wood, who stole
whomever he wanted and, with a flint,
gave them three incisions one palmo wide
and two long in the sides, then pulled
out their entrails, cut off a piece to throw
into the fire, made three cuts
in the arm, the second in the *sangradura*
obverse to the elbow, dislocated it before
setting everything back in place, hands
touching the wounds and saying they were healed
      Sometimes he would appear at their dances,
in costume, dressed as a woman or a man,
and whenever he wanted to he picked up
the *buhío* house, lifted it into the air,
then dropped it with a crash
      The food they offered him
he never ate, and when they asked
him where he was from, he pointed
to a cleft in the earth

After the Avavares told us all this
we laughed, but then they brought us
many of whom he had taken, and we saw
the scars of the cuts on their sides
exactly in the manner they had described
and we told them not to worry
for the One God would protect them

John

Bartlett, Rhode Island bookseller
surveys the southern border, 1850
(48,000 slaves in the young state)
for Uncle Sam's Boundary Commission
separated from family for 2½ years
to tend to astronomical observations
through sextant, chronometer, telescope
measuring the occultations of stars by the moon
points connected by chain and compass
meteorological registers kept, set aneroid
and ordinary barometers, maps plotted
one inch to a mile, magnetic topography recorded
through crisis to crisis, the Commission
collects animals, fish, plants, minerals,
fossils, more than twenty native languages,
vocabularies noted, ethnologized
manners, customs, arts, sketches of people, scenes,
landscapes, flora and fauna, cave art,
along the way, read Erman's *Travels in Siberia*,
visited copper mines, met Chipota,
a Lipan chief ("*Mucho frio—poco de viskey*?"),
watched four of the Commission's teamsters hang
for murder, provided Mexico with more land
than Congress allowed, through stretches of
"exceedingly monotonous" country, "inhospitable
wilderness," encamped on the margins, suffered
hunger, heatstroke, fatigue, thirst, long illness
["that they embraced a voluntary Exile
in a Squalid, horrid *American* Desart" (Mather)],
that Mexicans trapped and killed 150 Apaches,
that American scalp-hunters had lured Apache
families with goods to trade before opening fire,
and while bedridden in Ures, December 23:

At the first fire of his men six Apaches were killed, and one was left by his companions mortally wounded. This man sat alone on the plain near a tall petahaya, the blood trickling from his wound and gasping for breath; but at the same time, clenching in his death-grasp his full drawn bow. His pursuers were thus kept at bay, knowing the certainty with which an Apache warrior marks his victim. The Opates were all armed with muskets or escopettes; and they discharged no less than ten shots at the dying Indian, not one of which took effect. At length an Opate lad of sixteen boldly advanced with his gun to within a short distance of the wounded man. The quick eye of the Apache was fired on his antagonist as he approached him. The young Opate levelled his gun and quickly pulled the trigger. The Apache at the same instant let fly the never-failing and deadly arrow, which, skimming over the plain, buried itself deeply in the neck of the warrior boy, and laid him dead on the spot. The ball of the Opate was equally sure. Both were slain.

> From the first of Bartlett's two-volume *Personal Narrative*
> of crossing the sandy desert plains through thick
> *mezquit chapporal*, sparse tufts of grass, down to
> Acapulco, where he stays at the Canton Hotel, "the very
> perfection of neatness," run by Quanahu, son
> of the Celestial Empire:

The landlord had long lived on the coast, and spoke Spanish well. Of English he knew nothing. His attendants, who were all Chinese, wore their native costumes. Mr. Quanahu, like most foreigners who settle in the country, had taken to himself a Mexican wife, a genteel pretty-looking woman. During the evening, this lady, with a number of her young female friends, took their seats at one of the refreshment tables, and seemed to enjoy themselves mightily over their wine, cakes, ice-cream, and dulces; while Mr. Quanahu and his Chinese waiters supplied their wants as carefully as those of any of his guests.

> Rides a mail steamer back to San Diego, along the way,
> passes a whaleship 16 months out from New Bedford,
> they trade newspapers for a large turtle, fevers spread
> on board, a Cornish passenger dies, Methodist minister
> prays over the body before they launch it into the sea

Estevanico

of Azamor
at the mouth of the Oum er Rbia River
Province, Doukkala
Dorantes' slave, with Captain Castillo
and myself Álvar Núñez Cabeza de Vaca
named in honor of Alhajahad
grandson to the conqueror of Canaria,
four far from a tribe, lost
band of followers, at once
master and slave, trader and healer
lost, after shipwrecks, having starved,
our thirst so great we drank salt
as foretold by the Muslim woman from Hornachos
We sought war and gold and souls
among the barbarians, burned their villages,
then separated, lost, but in the end escaped
by the mercy *en la pasión de nuestro redentor Jesucristo*
to tell the tale of the Seven Cities of Cíbola
      The hunger and thirst we endured
the people always cured, whatever they had they gave
us, warmed us by their fires, sheltered us
      People who mourned their dead children
for a year, each morning before sunrise,
the whole clan wept, noon and at daybreak,
household didn't eat for three months,
so deep is their mourning for their children
      People of the bison, men naked, women
and elders clothed in deerskin, the land parched,
maizeless, they boiled their water with hot stones, we
headed into the setting sun, following the maize road,
surviving each day on a handful of deer fat,
crossed the river, to the people who only ate polvos
de paja, *powders of grass*, for four months of the year,
they gave us flour and squash and frijoles and cotton

mantles, we crossed the medranos, the people
gave us beads and coral and emerald arrowheads
      We saw women in lengths of cotton, closed
with ties in the front, half-sleeves of buckskin
that touched the ground, and wearing shoes
The people sought our blessings, thought
we came from the sky, Estevanico
speaking for us, as we passed
through a great number of diverse languages,
we knew six, but found a thousand differences
      We were fed on the hearts of deers,
some feared and fled from us, the people
having been chained by the ones who came before us,
the ones we sought so feverishly to tell them
No more killing
No more chains, please
Do no more harm, Holy Majesty,
the wretched and disastrous end
we suffered on account of our sins

■

In the Book of Last Words
Clifford Phillips says before his execution,
"Certainly murder cannot be an instrument of Allah."

Reading

Shelter from the hurricane
In the forest by the Rio Grande
The boy and his equipage gone
Cataract torrent below
The fallen-tree bridge, across
The fissure, chasm, gully,
Up the heights of the rock
Steps hewn by some human art
Into the limestone hollow, there
The missionary finds a fire
Of burning brands, plantains,
Calabash of rum, garments, banja,
Weapons and provisions
For runaway slaves, *every island's*
But a prison guarded by sea, he
Roasts some jerk hog, eats, drinks,
Dreams, incarcerated sensorium,
Her death in his arms, wakes
To the figure before the lamp
Obeah caretaker of the cave
In a poncho, red-silk turban,
Host and guest, master or slave,
Their cavernous exchange
What future plans, what hinted rebellion
Has fate conjured together
What secret purpose, the white powder
What knowledge does it divine
White as the snows of Mount Atlas
The obeah rubs onto the priest's
Fingers, which turn as crimson as
The setting sun in a storm, flows
Like blood down his arm, deep, so deep,
The bloodshed of the innocent

Poetry

Overtones   aggregate relevance
like the *nous*   of Anaxagoras   whirling aether and air
disperse   through a tear in the clouds
a long glance   seared in the cells
Lines surface   cluster
a mountain   a sail   the flash
of a roadrunner tail   along the unmoving canyon trail
longing   for what appears   unclear
in a vision   of the unseen

In the Book of Last Words
Anaxagoras of Clazomenae says,
"Give the boys a holiday."

The Lights

One night we sought out the Lights
off an empty highway, not a soul but us four
on some version of the No Tour
among others brought here before and after
by a gift, dropped into a bracket of words
listening to the cosmic noises in the night
And on the horizon we saw the Lights, hovering
eerily for a moment, chills at being chosen, growing
brighter then disappearing, reappearing, following
the curves, we realized, of the distant road
We waited longer in the darkness
There must have been stars but I can't remember any
Then lights on the highway slowly neared us
on the divide, closer, closer, the lights
of the Luciferum pulled round
blinding us, a patrolman stepped out
asked us what we were doing here
in the middle of nowhere, alone
on the highway in the middle of the night,
he searched our car, paced to and fro,
scanning our faces with a bitty flashlight,
dispatcher's voice abruptly beckoned
over the radio, saving us for a moment,
the patrolman spoke a few words in a low voice
then walked back toward us with a last question,
"You all're Americans aren't you?"
And we lied and said "Yes"
And he nodded and turned, told us
to keep out of trouble before
hitting the leather, and drove off
While in my mind I could feel
the Gunslinger's stare, the grave
cold look he cast at me
from the saloon seat next to me
when he tried to warn me: "This
is a desert full of *fucking*
agents who want to *fuck* you."

Stra

Gunslinger Stra steps into the bar
and asks me if I have any last words.
I say, "No . . . ," but then he shoots me
(with his open fingers of course).

Stra

Gunslinger Stra confides in me
over two tumblers of liquor, mine
Bushmills with rocks, his straight
from the eagle's mouth, voice a low whisper,
"I actually practice nonviolence. No
other way out of the quagmire we're in,
you know, exceptionalism, the connected
collective . . . I sold my last escopetas
to an old lady with a springer spaniel.
And the police, well, let them lay
down their arms, like the Brits or Down
Under, and then keep 'em off the streets,
no strappin' a piece about town
to be pulled out on a whim and a fancy,
no more end-of-days mentality, machismo
delusions of security against the state,
when we are said state, one endless
teachable moment, schools safe . . . "
[at this point, his sky-blue eyes glassed
over as he fondled his empty holster]
" . . . compassion, more compassion
it's true, but is it enough to need
liebe Erde, who asks nothing in return?
The soul hardens into a gun."

Stra

Gunslinger Stra traces his maternal roots
to the hidden puerto Zicatela on the south coast
of Oaxaca. His features are of a weathered
nordique, wind-beaten, ruddy Cherokee, dolichocephalic
face a manifest, as the saying goes, of the heart's
invisible furies. I ask
if he's spent much time south of the border.
With a slight drawl he replies, "La experiencia poética
es un abrir las fuentes del ser. Un instante
y jamás. Un instante y para siempre."
High-voltage vape swirls in a purplish haze
above a posse of happy hipsters, a moth
flutters near a filament flame, circles away,
opening up a wellspring of being, an
instant and never. An instant and forever.

Stra

Gunslinger Stra stares at me
from the mirror behind the bar-
tender, eyes aglint beneath his rolled brim
night dims complicit within our accord
filling us like the holy ghost, one body
reaching for what the scholastics called
habitus, the inner form and spiritual wake-
fulness that activates an ethos, in the hour
of our deepest neediness, the shared
silence after the last song on the jukebox
(Albert Ayler Trio, *Spiritual Unity*, track three)
and the loneliness of parting beneath the stars.

Stra

Gunslinger Stra talks dirty on his stool:
"I freely confess . . . a natural attraction
toward our black brethren, though chances
being scarce in this town, *nitimur in vetitum*,
Houston beckons on occasion." I blink;
the night's as early as our acquaintance.
I couldn't tell if he'd be a wolf or a sheep
in the field, slipping between one
cliché to the next, beauty's brief gasp,
what drives our predilections, suburban
moods more missionary in practice,
he sallies forth on early "Calamus,"
the sweet flag of Walt's disposition, "If
only Black Lucifer had gotten in on the action
of his scented herbage, it would amalgamate
a truly intimate ideal. But still we
extend his *Leaves* through acts of conquest,
roaming earth's amplitude, latigo pulled tight,
riding high on the horn, rustling, hustling."

Stra

Gunslinger Stra paints "artifacts" on scraps of wood,
"a dabbler in the landscape," he says of himself, "like
how Boccaccio described Giotto's *umiltà* before nature,"
though adds that he only paints stuff he remembers,
ingrained, "not to fix a memory, but to stretch
unfamiliarity with a place," he misquotes a beloved
painter, then adds, "a natural place in my mind,
that is, the paint not alienated from the real, though
when I make a tree, I don't choose a tree . . . my tree is
one that doesn't exist, with no preconceived aesthetic,"
this being no conceit, no ars poetica reformulated,
apparently, he tried to compose directly, *en plein air*,
but the result always "came out like starched laundry,"
his lack of technical-compositional know-how just that,
a lack, whereas through memory's filter of a line, a face, a
pile of rubble at dusk, patch of dried grass by a bucket,
a calf, old utility pole, shadows of sails, bars of light in
grainy graphite and oils, he could blindly lift the veil
from the world and bridge the abyss that yawned
within him, laceratingly, spontaneously, with little
deliberation, "skipping the Torah to mainline the Kabbalah"
"a kind of reverse blind contouring, my eyes
fixed on the page, painting being the dramatic action
in the course of which reality finds itself split apart"
"I work like nature," Stra strides, "without imitation, while
on cold, lonesome nights, I use the artifacts for kindling."

Stra

"Marfa is no arid La Jolla, no Palm Springs decoy,"
Stra holds forth, "no, not even a crude tract of La Mancha
(though lance a windmill here and you'll be shot
faster than you can say Alifanfaron), this place is
perceived as a small cosmopolitan oasis, celebrated
for its current industry: art. Art as external creative force, more
careful development. Mather's Squalid *Desart*. An art-
island that depends on poor locals and neighboring islands
to keep costs down, and while not as shaka as Moloka'i,
there's no hurry or rush, rather it's one contained
speed trap, push the gas and you'll find yourself at the pink
courthouse, begging at the bench of Judge Cinderela, who'll
take cash for not changing your Prius into a pumpkin.
Emigrants, illegals, crewelers and crafters, adobe-
mixers, daytrippers, homesitters, hydroponic tomato pickers,
ranchers, loners, passing celebrities and photoshooters (if
passing quickly), registered sex offenders (if not offending),
poets and failures, javelina sausage-makers, bond-makers, readers
and home-birthers, all make up the local fix, a place of few
first words, desperado bookishness, no public playground, kids
scarce public schools on a downswing, low-rent housing
harder to come by as out-of-towners buy and sell and buy,
population wavers around two thousand, 70%
Obama voters, most common surname Sanchez
or Martinez, pick your plot: Latino or Anglo,
bookstore's to die for, ditto the radio station, cozy library,
camp in a trailer, eat Mediterranean in a trailer, drool
over Ramona's burritos, chains scarce mind clears,
leave your pretense at the Prada, a quiet simplicity
settles in, to start anew or continue to lose
your way and loose your imagination farther out
to Presidio's giant battery reserve. . . ." Stra pauses,
tosses back his Mezcalero, and I notice the scar
running across the gular skin of his throat. "But hey,
Marfa, what do I know, I just got here, tomorrow
hasta pronto—an airstrip would kill you."

Thirteen Preparatory Drawings of the Substation Grid from Marfa to Presidio

"By force of looking and working nature becomes concentric."
—Rackstraw Downes, quoting Cézanne in
"Turning the Head in Empirical Space"

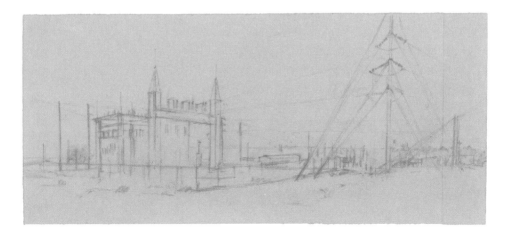

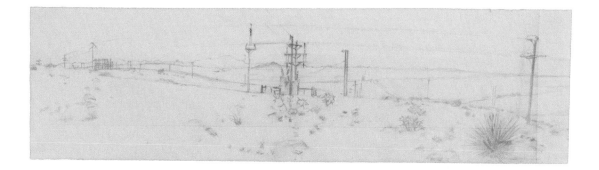

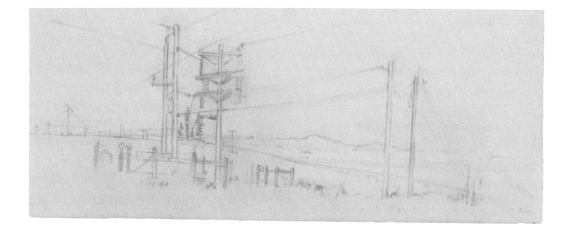

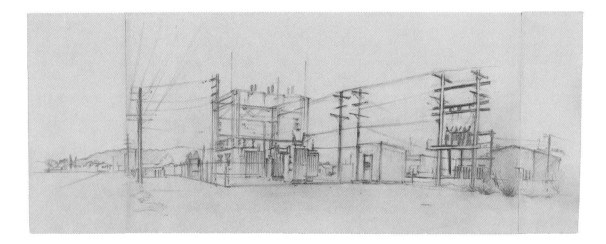

Thirteen Stations

I.
Chasing the light, by the light of the real
looking into the "continuous enveloping

sphere," at the gate-towers, the "calligraphy
of the wires," conveying the light between

earth and air, lines pulled to the poles
inscribed in the field, high and near, far

and low, circle the edges, paper
strips stretch grid over grid, drawn

further into the world, manifesting site

II.
Will we disperse into particles of light?
Listening to the splendor of the light?

At the readymade ruin, temple
without altar, spires hidden in

public view, empty appearances

Purpose bared pure
function in structure

engineered desert
resonance

high voltage danger zone

where "spontaneous facts"
leap into sight and lines
channel the energy currents

to look anew
test the vantage points
question the assumed, as far

as the eye can see graphite
make way for a warm, flat sheet

III.
Pencil's lightness to fingers, paper's
lightness to pencil, fingers' lightness

to mind, mind's lightness to heart
air's lightness to paper, knowing

within the formal limits
motion's lightness to touch

the identity of grass, the energy of sun

IV.
Balance the scale
from tangent to square

shadow to air, rhythm
to volume, where

to stand
a little more east

than the day before, a little closer
to the beaming faces, two

or three steps more
north, head tilts better

to position the poles, slow the lines

alive because you have the vision of what it is in
front and where it goes behind at the same time

traced faintly through sky

above the residence
south on the incline

Twin cylinder tanks
at rest at the margins

Chain-link emptiness

V.
Music in the lines
pattern the heavens

A stave soars over the rails
neume pitches polyphony
keyed to the analog relays

set frames, variations
on a scene perceived

Less indefinite
draft closer to being

incomplete, red threads
square mat to dome, lead
dust trails leaving

king's blue light
gamboge lake

titanium white wisps
brushed raw sienna earth

VI.
At the sixth station, the parabolic reflection,
the houses in the middle of the sphere

Piranesi *veduta* of the Colosseum

Boundaries fuse with electricity, nature
with human nature, protective hub

A trinity of breakers curve in the beams
on the groundless ground to the fading

periphery, inside the machinery, close-
up inside the energy of the machinery

to recompense the parched eternities of the desert

Conquered by the light, far from the slag
heaps, generating station with ibis and egret

behind, salt shed ahead, vertical interior sky-
lights of the studio East, south of Houston

VII.
The lines have brought us here

Out in the open desert
among the low hills we've
settled, town to town

Each plot for sale, each acre

peaceful breakers
wave particles
        of sand
sting the eyes

Atop the wooden crossarms

shapes metes
and bounds materialize

the concrete, empirical
series, "by force

of looking" at the discrete

components
of the actual object

elsewhere distant, foreground
extends land's height

series improvised *to a minimum,*
as if to prove that necessities can be found
that are as beautiful in their consequences

as contingencies can prove to be

Across topography grasped
essentials of the whole relation

meaning enfolding space

VIII.
Through shattering sun, off the access road
trail hiked from desert defile to scree plateau

Mule-pack materials lugged to the chosen site

Thirst physical, eyes wind-dried, back ache bent
brokenness, hour after hour standing in the rain-

shadow hills, looking for the light-cast perfection
on a cholla stem . . . "the color more luminous as it

approaches" . . . gestures of Barbary fig, creosote shrub
Drought-resistant substation, anonymous presence

IX.
Power lines radiate up from a cross
Rays of light shine down from above

Utility's long march in the wilderness

Slow swell sand tracks merge at the ninth
station, current caravan cohabitation

X.
"Countless signals lost with a photograph,"
Stra replies. "Wondrous conduits interconnect
the senses, I paraphrase, and the camera is no eye,
no . . . not even a lazy one; it can't see, it links no brain, no
emotion in the consistent instant, the info it relates
cannot replace the experience of seeing, drawing
the world in the open, with no mistakes but choices,
carefully observed, vital key to the practice, a plain
practice of breaking habits, with fertile traditions,
like Courbet at Trouville. . . .
But next season, if you go to the place where the track
splits into three, reiterated pole in a 'V,'
you'll still find his Jullian plein-
air foldable easel prints marked in the dirt."

XI.
A brief century
of power, the grid

grown

dependent upon
so much, our

wants
for nothing

anything
but blackout, please

little substation

perched on a bedrock knoll
safeguarding the lines

Light up the night . . . !

Of the poem

arriving as if by telepathic
electricity

"not built out of words . . .

makes the words and
contains their meaning"

Your soul
dwells in the portrait

XII.
Looking west toward the mountains

sun's arc at midday, gaze itinerant arc
of a track, arc of a mesa, arc of the poles

distilled in the contours of chroma's absence

Lines bind things to the light
No two wires alike

Trusses heavy with lead

rub onto the hand's
underside, eraser

jackknifes down the elevation
from Marfa to Presidio
sand paper lowlands

No fixed edges or intervals, as R. notes *In
re Pain sans mie*, gaze itinerant focus round
the Chihuahua plains, remote subsistence

Circling space in the fading duration

XIII.
With patience particulars of site
reveal themselves in winter light

Counterpoint pursued Bach
to his deathbed, the *cantus firmus*

he had heard thirty years ago
reemerged in the chorale *Vor*

deinen Thron tret' ich hiermit, his last
unfinished song, a fragment made

up of four melodic fragments from
his earlier prelude *Wenn wir in höchsten*

Nöten diminished, inverted, developed
contrapuntally through four voices

keyed toward G major, as grace falls
in thirds, rises the bars breath figures

before the lines appears the throne

In the Book of Last Words
Jane Addams says, "Always.
Always water for me."

■

In the Book of Last Words
Charlie Livingston says before his execution,
"You all brought me here to be executed,
not to make a speech. That's it."

■

In the Book of Last Words
Emily Dickinson says,
"I must go in, the fog is rising."

Sod

Each day, at the hottest hour
the lady's sprinklers turn on
to water her squared patch of lawn

Turf green bracketed between
plots of low chroma, friable yard, a
desert dream of sod sushi-baran

.

Epigraph to *Desert Passages* from *Voss*:
"Deserts have been shown to resist
history and develop along their own lines."

.

A mirage of sameness
dispelled, each sand-
grain a snowflake, each
desert distinct epoch to biome,
each sunset heaven displaced,
each memory absquatulates
from arid vacancy to a margin
of safety, from profundity
to mortality, from tragedy to
micro-algae salinity, promise
of configurative energy

No place

worn of words

only worn words
to be mourned, patient

of being reborn, chronotoped,
loved and known *locus amoenus*

ksana and kalpa, reworn
garmented worth radiates

warmth, aeolian raiment
showering threads of silver, lilac

soaking desert caliche, gestant
commonplace mesa, cedar brake

Substation

Crossing the land's long swell in the desert
More earth than sky, low peaks soft horizon glow
Like a mirage of the future, fine sea-green flecks

Movement in stillness, shades drink the air, no
More escarpments of swaying grass here spangled
With endless varieties of flowers, as Byron

Saw the *enamelled lawn* on the way up the range
To the Kampirak pass, *edged by clouds above*
And the ever-receding waves of Turkestan below . . .

Blue chicory, tall pink hollyhock-mallows, clumps of lemon-
Coloured cornflowers on stout brown knobs, patches of low white
Spikes like jasmine, a big spotty-leaved saxifrage, a small flower

Of butter yellow with a brown inside like garden musk, bunches of blue
And pink nettles with stingless leaves, and branching sprays of rose-
Pink lobster-blossoms, not flowers but stones winking at us

From this liminal expanse where all water's hidden, stored
In the morning-star leaves of the single yucca leaning
Toward sunbeams, bursts of nolina tufts, cholla coral dried

Tarbush, and the felled trees, trucked, raised from the dead
Into purgatory, limbless giants, re-limbed, stabilized in wind
Burdened utility arrested, blending into the shallow seas

Of dust, bedded to the trails on their slow exodus past
The ephemeral streams to the terrestrial city, standing tall
In their servitude to power, attenuated, the costs of which

We choose to assume, dissemble, consequences connect
Lines of sight we cannot detect from a distance, clouded
by assumptions, habits, speed, inattentive to the physical

Nature of the mineral sand, yellow-edged agave spears,
Aeolian vibration, dab of blue-gray by the cross-
Road, faint circle of ash, strewn shells adobe petals

Like a mirage of the future, fine sea-green flecks
More earth than sky, low peaks soft horizon glow
Crossing the land's long swell in the desert

The Grass

Bouteloua black
     grama grass red
chino side-
oats blue grama grass
     hairy buffalo-
     grass toboso threeawn
land's dawn 旦 sun
over sand, tumble
wind-
     mill witch- cup- saltgrass
plains love- indiangrass, prairie
cordgrass, pink pappusgrass, sprangle-
     top green knotroot
     bristle, bluestem, tangle-
head, sacaton
panicles
     open, golden drop-
seed blooms desert winter-
     grass, awns twist, un-
twist, *such*
syllables flicker
     out of grass
       : Nanissáanah
thirst, ghost dance
     native
spirits, active
roots, footstalks
to soil as to site, stems
     bend, range-
     lands wave, seiche
fields sway, clouds
pass over-
     grazed grass
staked, fenced

            dries, weakens, dies,
fallen
      crowns, the grasslands
what
      comes to pass, ranch-
hand lands, live-
      stock livelihood
wildlife gone, displaced, migrations
impeded, scales im-
balanced
      the years
          spread, each *itself*
hitched to everything else
in the universe
      nodes
          hollowed, drought-
land years, drops
      on the hardpan
            nature
is endless
         regeneration
trichloris, muhly, switch-
grass, wind misses
      沙 沙 *shasha* through the pass-
es, whispering seeds
         will pass, will pass
      within leaves
listening
      grasses, *not only*
the revelation
but the nature behind
      to sustain it, over-
land grasses seeds
spread and grow, rhizome,
stolon to sod, curly
      mesquite cotton-
      top, draft

to draft 草
ten thousand
        grasses, 草 dancing
culms 草 of grass
florescence, sheaths
and blades whorl
flower to
        flower, wild
                grass, knowing
wind strips, slips
of time, the leaves
words weave, un-
        weave the
grass

In the Book of Last Words
philologist Joseph Wright says,
"Dictionary."

■

Yoruba Ladder

ara   body or matter

ará   part or relation; inhabitant of a place

àra   form or custom; repetition of a journey

ara   at all

àrá   loud thunder

arà   a kind of bird

àrà   wonder

Javelinas

There the javelinas go
Through the brush, quick
As horses, on their toes

Toward the fiery-orb, day's
Last ray round the spiral
Center, bar of stars, they roam

In herds, for roots and forbs,
Grubs and prickly pear, what
Arid comfort, unassuming airs,

Nub of a tail, hooves tramp
Scrub, a litany of huffs, teeth
Clack, snouts twitch, eyes glint

Glassy-black, mane and musk,
Fangs and dusk, what shadows
Rush along the rings of grass

To blaze trails of light and ash

Lechuguilla

It can take twenty years
for the agave lechuguilla
to bloom and seed, maize-
yellow anthers, perched
like commas atop crimson
filaments, hang ten in the air
around the lone
panicle
stalk, giant
hummingbird tongue
bends to sky
from the mouth of a spiny
star body, rooted to earth, wildly
suckering rosettes, fruit sets once
a lifetime, the lechuguilla
flowers for maybe four days
before it dies
only to be
reborn
as a clone
off-
shoots choice toxic juice
for javelinas

Like the land of the lost
driving down to the old fort
Pterodactyls
in the air
really glossy
ibis, passers-by
watering in the pool
at the center of the flat crater
orbiting the air, returning to water

■

Sand ash-
pebble leaps
up, flattens
down, invisible:
spider

Hey, Marfa, you're too far out to turn into Soho, combination Pizza Hut and Taco Bell, your slow-circling unexpected crossroads, boundless space bound by water-flow, your phony bank as art foundation, phony gas station pizza foundation, reinventing the old into new-world social distortions, ongoing nouveau aesthetic western, second-home settlers exchanging spare economies for more amenities, daycare, smoothies, longtime residents struck by the desert music, strangers listening to air, dancing to Yacht, mind's endless mosaic, spirit needing illumination, from the outside looking farther out, night sky's brilliant Aldebaran, bull's fiery eye burning with forgetting.

There are moments of feeling

as if this town arranges itself
under a glass vitrine, as you

walk, the public assembles
somewhere out of sight

like a Fourier phalanstère
without apartments, hidden

share of passional attractions
impossible to partake of

Biked past my neighbor the burro
crossed the tracks down the hill
past Pueblo Market to the south-
side, past some HUD units,
the Blackwell School
closed eleven years after Brown
v. Board of Ed., past
Hector and Ester's white-
washed tree trunk
where the Virgin Mary once appeared
at night, illuminated through the trees,
to the former castrum, home to
refugees, border patrol,
chemical warfare battalion,
Women Army Corps, army airbase,
a POW camp for Germans
turned art foundation artillery shed
Zutritt fuer unbefugte verboten
stenciled on brick above a doorway
having reached Thunderdome
last outpost colony of site-specific art
in a warehouse lined with squared-and-quartered
windows, evenly spaced with 100 interior
variations of equally proportioned aluminum
rectangle-cubes, ranked row upon row
gridded cement, waist-level shiny
reflections, frame echoing framed
emptiness, desert mirage refuge
as if a Gregorian score translated
into mini-HUD units to look through
at the Egyptian sands, and arrive
once more, somewhere around G major

J. Chamberlain

Lots of accidents

stabilizing this tau-
       crossed room
of adobe
shade, spaced

out with crumpled cars
Upon the concrete seal

float squares of light
sun-thaw, snow unsealed

C. Andre

Line of wood blocks
splits the room, ends
      at twin door-
way, light
runs round a corner, tin
      ribbon unspools
metal plates make
a path to
      a pack of camels
through the eye
of a needle, leans on a wall
      Earth's gravity
outside steel
bands rest flat
      across ochre-
red speckled gravel
fills a courtyard
      bound by roofed
passages, wood posts
hollow out the metric
      pattern
garden rectangles
weather the latitude
      face to the skies
beds bloom, lines
on a page, rust
      becomes form
structure place, marble
slaves stand on, *contrapposto*
      water's memory
redox, slowly corrodes
to dust, unfinished
      words preserved
under glass materiality
particles, rest unsure

Particles of Irwin

Southwest desert   a place
              with the least
identifications or connotations

         you   go along
for a long while   nothing seems
              to be happening

   all   flat desert   can
take on   sort of

     I mean   takes on

   an almost   magical quality

      stands up
hums

       becomes

        so beautiful

the presence   so   strong

twenty minutes   will

    simply

       stop

R. Horn

Crossed the threshold
with the desert sunlight

inside, almost empty room, swept
cement floor poured squared slabs

cracks, face wood rafters
X's overlap, barren walls

scraped blue residue, crumbling
plaster, more cracks, longhouse

windows squared in facing
double rows, drawn to two

copper artifacts, weigh down the
floor, obliquely strewn, smooth

polished circular faces, lopped off
horn-pair down, below the knees

there and here, ritual debris, what's
missing being complete, moving

between the threshold here
to there, where I am am I

to place this pair in dust in
air: synapse, isthmus, corpus

conduction each line relates
each pair upon pair mined

from the outcrop, reduced to spare
purified chunks, nonvisible waves

hum, as it happens again, double
rays curve the precise fabrication

Lorina Naegele, Judd's cook
and gardener, said on the radio,
"He brought me over here
and I never had seen art, okay,
so he brought me over here
and he showed me everything,
and I said, 'What is this?!'
And he said, 'That's art.'
And I said, 'Oh . . . ! Okay, well . . . '
That's when I started knowing
what art was. I had never seen it."

Grave

They said animals had dug up the artist's bones
so they reburied them deeper. Then the animals
dug them up again, so they reburied them deeper
still. The third time the animals dug up the bones,
they said they realized their mistake: that by
leaving the dead body on a remote plateau
for vultures to consume, and then wrapping
the skeleton with hessian strips before interring it
directly into the earth (all done as indicated in
the artist's will which, significantly, said nothing
about the possibility of reburial), they were,
per attribute,* essentially bound by nature's will
and so should follow (despite their further
disquiet) its designs to the very end. Only then
did they give the animals and elements free reign
over the bones, letting carpals and tarsals scatter
among stones, hooves crush vertebrae and ribcage,
coyote drag coxa to gully, dogs gnaw femur,
tibia, wind and rain sweep phalanges away,
and so on across the vast homestead, the artist's
skull slowly settling into its salt-rift disintegration,
while the grave remained empty, unfilled, unmarked
earth's epitaph, stoneless depths of the desert
wild waves cave to sea, sand to sea, wave to sea.

---

* Baruch Spinoza: *Per attributum intelligo id, quod intellectus de substantia percipit, tanquam ejusdem essentiam constituens* ("By attribute I understand what the intellect perceives of substance as constituting its essence").

Circle

in flip-flops
kicked a shin dagger, thorns
buried between toes, broke apart
tweezers, glue no use, wound
festered for days, illiterate
limp, horned-toad scuttle,
never take a shortcut drunk
through a dark desert yard
in flip-flops

Circle

within this luxury of time
I, myself fugitive subject-
witness and messenger,
do attest to the vitality that has
opened up a wellspring of being
within this luxury of time

Circle

In broad daylight
I first unearthed it
from *The Danish Notebook*
its epigraph itself un-
earthed from *Return to the Book*:
"The sun," noted Reb Gabbar,
"*is a flaming hoop which a little girl*
trundles around the earth. Nobody
has ever discovered the child
even though she plays
in broad daylight."

Fire

When the fire broke out I was translating Liu's *Elegies* as I had been doing each day since my arrival, trying to keep to a strict schedule as marked out on my calendar, counting down the days until the end of my stay which, if I remained vigilant, would coincide with a finished draft of the translation. Ample desk, printer, fax machine, Wi-Fi, an uncluttered, modern office that lacked no clip nor staple, no object out of place, the care and meticulous thought put into its congruent construction and arrangement all for the benefit of fortunate others. Every morning I'd open the blinds on the three sides of the study's floor-to-ceiling windows and feel the sunlight fill the room. Five years on words still verify the real. The familiar smell of a distant brush fire triggered a faint warning signal in my brain, but as I could see no clouds of smoke I thought nothing more of it. The phone rang in the afternoon. Douglas relayed the fire's latest news, saying there was no need to worry, he'd call again if any change. The next day I heard the whole town, in fact, had been on edge waiting for the call to evacuate. An abandoned house on the eastern outskirts had been swallowed by the flames, the wind then abruptly shifting, blowing the flames north toward the Davis peaks, danger by chance averted. How nature uncountenanced becomes contingent upon our own improvident history. Divine measure quickly recedes from view as the fire rages on, mocking any dream of self-sufficiency. I grew up in the arid climate of southern California. The dry Santa Ana winds, our harmattan, heavy gusts from beyond the mountains, would blow through the valley like Old Man Winter of the West, a devil in disguise, charging the air with a strange anticipatory light, watering our eyes with particles of dust and debris. I watched the fire that season through my father's binoculars, its start somewhere on the slope of the small mountain across the valley. The wind, as if casting a magic spell, suddenly caused the flames to leap through the air, from the far side of the dirt road across to a clump of brush on the nearer side—the flickering, flowing sleeves of a shaman, dancing. I inhaled a quick breath, lowering the binoculars from my eyes, shielding myself from danger. The fire spread along the ridge of the mountain through the night, transforming into the trembling spines of a dragon dividing from earth. The fire burned for days, moving farther north with the winds, the Chihuahua desert aglow with patches and rippling streaks of orange in the darkness, the air remarkably clear in town though the inescapable smell of smoke brought particles of ash with it that drifted through the door and window screens, covering the temporal surfaces of my amber chamber of light. The four of us drove up the highway, beyond the snake house, the fort, the secret petroglyphs, through the sawtooth hills, to gambol on the shores of Balmorhea, a cienega natural spring built by the Civilian Conservation Corps and the last known habitat of the Comanche Springs pupfish. We were the only visitors there until members of a young indie band showed up whom we recognized from their show the previous night. They docked themselves as far from us as possible, across the ethereal blue pool. What could ever replace water in this world, its sublime submissiveness? Like an endangered species we splashed in the healing outflow of the crystal-clear spring while columns of smoke gathered slowly skyward in the distance, a gentle Vesuvius releasing its concentric plume. I could make out a figure climbing the mast's rigging while Icarus drowns below. Watching the fire spread that night, feeling its hot breath from safety, its living, elemental presence, while neighbors stood entranced in the darkness, faces illuminated by the flames, fire trucks parked along the sloping roads, firefighters in full gear ready for the slightest shift in the wind to enforce an evacuation, I recognized its childlike power, its burning destruction and grace, its resolve to consume any substance or fiction. On our way back to town, we stopped the car by the side of the highway and walked into the middle of the scorched landscape, charred-black surface horizon covering the hills out beyond the lone observatory that still rose from the desolate landscape like Saint Paul's Cathedral after the blitz, as Rackstraw once described seeing it as a child. All around us stretched the abyssal strata of time turned up by the blazing plough, fertile black earth beneath our feet thirsting for rainfall, ready to begin again, to seed and sprout through the wax-sealed layers with renewed diversity, nature's timeless patience, desert's long native recovery unfurling bloom after bloom.

Poetry

Deposits cashed for   a living   floriation

■

In the Book of Last Words
Yolchi says to Sven Hedin
not far from Khotan-daria,
"Water, sir! Only a drop of water!"

Marfa Book Company

Tim & Caitlin sew the blue sail
at the center of Echo City

hoist Pythagoras's "friendship
makes the many one" with Sun

Congtian's "books occupy
the same position in the universe
as the soul does in the human body"

Cecilia

Thompson, the local
historian,
is almost blind, she
gives tours if you drive

Then winter arrived and she died

Her two slip-cased volumes
sit on my shelf, a third

one incomplete
soul

History

Take
no point of view
      for granted

And if you weren't
there to see it,
      the Opata reply,

"Sepore ma de ni thui"
"Perhaps you do
      speak the truth"

Dreams

Sharpied on a trash can
in the high-school bathroom:
"Where your dreams go"

Marmot

The desert is no place to hide for a human
A used car lot is no place to hide for a marmot

Now where

                                           nature grows   out of
the day's   realities   to please   human nature
        like a park   lines preserve   blur
   into nowhere   desert   existence   land's
scarcity   uncertain death   for man   dreaming
      westward nation   curving manifest   Memory's
   cadence   *more traces of history*   *than of growth*
     Nature claimed   compass redoubt   Trinity
   site   fallout   Forget-me-not   sea

In the Book of Last Words
Lorine Niedecker's mother B. P.
says to her, "Wash the floors ...
wash the clothes and pull the weeds."

In the Book of Last Words
Lorine Niedecker says to her husband,
" ... kiss ... kiss ... "

∎

In the Book of Last Words
Cary D. Kerr says before his execution, "Yes,
Tell my sister Tracey, I love you.
Nicole, thank you and I love you. Wanda and all of my friends,
I love you and thank you for your support.
To the State of Texas, I am an innocent man.
Never trust a court-appointed attorney.
I am ready Warden. Thank you, Brad, I'm sorry.
Check that DNA, check Scott. Here we go. Lord Jesus, Jesus."

∎

In the Book of Last Words
Françoise Gilot's grandmother says to her,
"Let me bathe myself in your eyes."

Tigie

One night at the Museum of Electronic Wonders, Tigie sat on the couch with me and we talked over gourmet grilled cheese—artichoke, jalapeños, gruyere with caramelized onions on sourdough—the room lined with space-age black-and-white TVs, retro radios, "Go West" mellowing to "The Sound in Your Mind" over the 8-track stereo. She wore the same straw hat and large leather work gloves she had worn when we had first met at Padres, where she was the oldest in the group by decades, as she was in this small crowd. Tigie chewed slow, breath a little short, eyes heterochromiac, one blue the other "cracked half brown and half blue, like a Catahoula cur" her friend Sterry later recalled. She faced me with a friendly smile, said she didn't sleep much, lived alone, talked about moving to New York after college, her fear of rattlesnakes allayed with shotguns, her horses, donkey poetry, cleaning both sides of the dishes, how she almost died once when her truck flipped over, and smiling, asked me, "So what do you think of this town?" and I replied glowingly, mouth salivating bliss, until someone came over to talk to her, and I said goodbye and walked back into the night. Two years passed until I saw her again, on Morley Safer's *60 Minutes* spot, she flashed by in a photograph on the screen—Tigie had died.

Grave

Among the makeshift crosses,
wood or metal, double-nailed
at the base, stone cairn rubble,

unmarked wolf graves, ghost town
silver rush boom to bust, of the past
or future pukará Atacama by the Río

Grande, this no fortress but bodies
offered to the mines, lives swallowed,
tunnels flooded, children anonymous

rock, rest in peace Tom Walkee (sic)

Cave

Raúl from Ojinaga
waits tables each day
then crosses the border back
home, where he was a geologist
He's now in his mid-fifties

We trek through the hills
of tuffaceous sandstone, igneous
Perdiz, into the Early Cambrian and
on through the Permian's inland seas

Foraminifera clades, Raúl finds
ecstatic, he leaps up and shouts
holding up a bivalve

Further into the bare heat
along veins of iron
past jellyfish in the rock
into the blackened cave

Circle

Two specks in a breadth of prairie
grass tall through objective lenses
camels grazing, at leisure in the wind
They speak to one another silently
of the old days enslaved by the US
Army, hauling survey expeditions,
protecting the frontier for destiny's
manifest, training for operations
against Apaches or Mormons, shuttling
salt and mail for Confederate troops,
suffering illness, whippings, abuse
how they arrived in this new world
with their foreign smell and blobbish head,
called names like "noble and useful brutes,"
the experiments and tests lasting roughly
a decade, until the War Department
judged them impractical, and on to the next
chapter: the pageant of the auction block
One rubs its generous lips against the other's
neck, as they speak of stories passed down
of circuses and races, packing for prospectors,
of being let loose to wander the strange
empty range, alone, their silent words leap
farther back, to dark sea-crossings,
the howling gales, a death, three births
on board, what life would be living
through them, in their native Levantine lands,
or Alexandria, or Kusadasi, as beasts of burden,
wrestling spectacle, kiddie ride, while now,
here, half-wild on a ranch, to breed
or not to breed, one stoops its head down,
and with a forefoot marks the sand
They speak to one another silently
camels grazing, at leisure in the wind
grass tall through objective lenses
two specks in a breadth of prairie

Fold

K. took us to the canyon
down through the wash
where Appalachia meets the Rockies
glass scarps above alkaline flats
succulent blossoms, curved-teeth leaves
pyrrhuloxia on a bow-dark tree, road
runner's moment's notice, no wasted sweetness
for the light-bearing hummingbird
A woman hiking with crutches
called down to us from a ridge, gestured
to the stone tchotchkes she had painted
arranged like icons among the rocky crevices
jagged with wind and time, water
and kitsch, matter of habitus animi
animal faces in the niches, on the metamorphic walls
watching our passing with devilish delight
She bade farewell and hobbled into sunlight
Desert spring cold splash, G. first then me
(fold) three a figure of sun (fold), L.'s eyes half-
closed (fold) day's heat fast disappearing, winter's
company feels like summer leaving, lush
river road border between folds

Substation

Scrub brush colonies of colorless sea urchins
Migrate up the slope, sparse sponge-weed
Shore curves to crest, beyond the three

Presiding poles turn the wires in a rough
Arc round the open cube, tensioned cables
Majestic masts sky-cloth Van de Graaf canon

Seeing perception in the charged articulations
Golden sections, taut topology backlit clouds
Thin white lines parallel in-and-out of view

Air of Bach's Third Suite
in the *Ária Brasileiras*
so sweet so sweet *the dreaming*
sky, falling syllables falling lines
      Eros in the light in the eyes
      between
notes, Angel of Victory
embolada songbird
scaling the sixteenths
2/4 heights
      Irerê of the Cariri forest
      Little wren dove oriole
seedcatcher flycatcher
thrush! *Canta mais! Canta mais!*
Of what was and the dawn
Of happiness and the beautiful
      heart . . . gone . . . now gone . . .
      moto perpetua moon
wanders over the border
enfolded by amethyst clouds
and flights of dust, luzerno fields
desert combs of grass
      cantilena *lá . . . liá . . . liá . . . ai . . .*
      Where does your song go?

E. Hernández

Wind bears
the sound of tinkling bells
     faint
river bluff
goats by the hide-site
Stone eclogue
    : Esequiel

Triesitas

These are the girls of the Asociación de "Triesitas" de Marfa, Tex., clothed in short white-hooded dresses, dress shoes and white, dark, or striped stockings, little faces reflecting somber quietude, surrounding a banner of Nuestra Señora de Guadelupe on the day of the Feast of the Immaculate Conception, photograph 1929: First row: Otelia Tercero, Tita Fierro, Margarita Armendarez; Second row: Socorro Magyanes, Socorro Mendias, Maria Menda, Juana Deanda, Margarita Gracia, Luisa Oroco, Rosalia Salgado, Eva Mendias, Rosa Oroco, Trina Borunda; Back row: Juana Rivera, Manuel Oroco, Lupe Ortega, Jesus Juarez, Carmen Almendor, Esperanza Mendias, Lola Ontiveros, Maria Viscaino, Julia Almendor.

In the Book of Last Words
Gary Graham says before his execution,
"I did not kill Bobby Lambert.
I'm an innocent black man that is being murdered.
This is a lynching that is happening in America tonight."

■

In the Book of Last Words
Jonathan Green says before his execution,
"I'm an innocent man. I did not kill anyone.
You all are killing an innocent man.
My left arm is killing me. It hurts bad."

■

In the Book of Last Words
Vincent van Gogh says,
"La tristesse durera toujours."

To be

freed
of the guillotine

the noose the ax
the poison gas the cross

To be freed of the boats
the stones the ring of fire

of the firing squad

To be freed of the breaking
wheel

the lethal
injections electric chair

the scaffold the stake the chamber
the stage

of the accepted progression
of the self-defeating system

To break the circle
for another sphere

in our collective existence
no mandate's immutable

for the unproven state

to cultivate innocence
without the engine of execution

The prisoner

of conscience
          cannot speak for his wife   She
     cannot be reached   at her apartment
her silence   a matter of governance
     by violence   the force of law   that silences
          any whistling   on the unspoken wind
Gray   paper scroll   wrapped
                    around a wooden core
found in a cave   centuries old   diamond
     words   she copies   over   and over
          a star at dawn   *a bubble in a stream*
               a flash of lightning   *in a summer cloud*
          a flickering lamp   *a phantom*   *a dream*
     Over and over   day   night   more night
          than day   awake   in the arrested room
she
     cannot leave   alone   she has   been silenced
          disappears   into the shadows   against the walls
     ritualized dolls   shadows   as if strangers   come from afar
          to observe   an image   smoke   or breath
float   out the window   open   sky   Until the
     moment
               nowhere   when that other life
     the one that lives through your life   stuffed
          with straw   stalled   at the precipice
     breaks down   systems   collapse   cells   necrose
ash-heap   afterlife   Phosphorous   particles
          drift   into Yellow Sea   drop   after
     drop   merges   grief   stretches out
its dark   infinite wings   and encloses   your still
          rose 霞 glow
                    霞

                         at the horizon
     with a new name   hollowed   of fate

116

Upon the hour

        of departure   the soul
     begins   to be freed   from the body's
ligaments   begins to reason   like herself
    (Browne avers)   and discourse in a strain
   above   mortality   within the fullness
of the life preceding   the breath
    at the center of consciousness   moves
toward the borders of consciousness   and words
    pass   into the living   song

Seashell for C. D.

Here was the sea
land's demise, the sands
my sleep, you shall be

As strong as my house
your breath will carry me
when the waters rise

On a more innocent shore
from your *one true and lonely word*
experienced against the hurt

Of other voices, breaking
the walls, waves passing through
me, desert's memory, salt blue

Pine for Paz

Ten thousand needles shimmer
against the light   liquid or ice
tufts cling to the branches   Sky-
ward   leaning   evergreen
: Sunstone memory

Reading

He died in the false dawn. The children
continued on with the boy's ghost

in the yucca wood they picked for fire
in the sun-warmed desert stones they chose

for their hearth, in the roots of the wondilla
grass and stalks of sugar cane they ate

for supper. Naked they walked along the stream as far
as they could go, then up the valley aglow with casuarinas,

creamy white bamberas, the pink of gums and eucalyptus,
up the slopes of mica and quartz, flecks of blue-green beryl,

their heat-dazed steps, sun swelling thirst, the salt-pans
a distant memory, bottle-green belts streaked with yellow

now a shimmering hum, blaze of butterflies swarming
up high in a rainbow cloud, they climbed, onto the crest,

looked down at the broad slab-sided rift, the mist
clearing to woodland, a slow-moving ribbon of water,

reed-lined, dotted with water birds, another country
the old woman stood under the stratocumulus layers,

unfolded the songmap, tracing the signs on the bark, each
pmere place revealed: broken line to circle, arcs, half-

moons, half-arrows, squares within squares, diamond and wave,
kuruwarri birthmarks, spirit children dreaming songs making,

remaking, awaran lightning struck the rock, Alhalkere nosepeg,
Piltawoldli possum house, Manaji potatoes, Tyimama sandhill

lines interlink site to Willunga-dust site, as it happened at
the windy place by the river Warriparinga: They say Kulutuwi

killed a tabu emu. His two half-brothers murder him. His uncle
Tjilbruke sees the sugar ants on the track carrying bits of bloody

hair, red ochre, and knows the brothers had lied when they
told him Kulutuwi had gone elsewhere to hunt, that in fact

they had killed him and the smoke-drying of the body
had already begun. And so in the evening, after the brothers

dance for him, after he sings the camp to sleep, Tjilbruke,
master fire-maker, surrounds their hut with morthibark

kindling and piles of grass, takes the iron-pyrite baruke and paldari
flintstone to light the tinder, crying out, "You are burning! Camp

on fire!" The brothers rush out and he spears them. Tjilbruke then
wraps his nephew Kulutuwi's body and carries him to the spring

at Tulkudangga beach to complete the smoking ceremony,
follows the route south down the coast, each place he rests he

weeps, his mekauwe tears seep into the ground, a new fresh-
water spring opens up, a new name springs forth: Karildilla

to Tainbarilla to Karkungga to Wirruwarrungga to Witawodli
to Kongaratinga to Patpangga, and at Yankalilla, the place

of falling apart, he finds a cave for Kulutuwi, lays him down
in the hollow dark depths of the cave, he walks deeper into

the cave, he passes through the many mouths of the cave, comes
out far inland covered in yellow dust that he shakes off as yellow

ochre, he walks on to Lonkowar to spear a gray currawong, rubs
its fat over his body, ties its feathers to his arms with hair-string,

and it happens: Kulutuwi leaves the earth for the sky, trans-
forming into tjilbruke, the glossy ibis, his body left behind

memorial martowalan outcrop rock, source of baruke
at Barrukungga, the place of hidden fire, cairn north

of Nairne in the Adelaide Hills, sun-veined vanishing-
lines, viatic tracks children follow home, tired but happy

In the Book of Last Words
Alonso Quixano the Good says,
"Ya no hay pájaros hogaño en los nidos de antaño"
"Yesterday's birds have flown from today's nest"

■

Errantly I wandered
through the golden groves
of Marfa à la Mancha

like you, idle reader, diverted
by idle moments, lost

to this idyll, unsound and flouted
order of economy, line's end

weighed and measured by the inner flame
words willed to burning on the arid plains

order of breadth in music,
idle listener, a painted image

no fiction could refrain, idle
viewer, caught as it were, between

lectura and *locura*, reading and
madness, its fruits of lawless reason
camerados for all seasons

Poetry

Incurable   and catching
disease   they said
in the days of the valiant
Knight of the Sorrowful Countenance
who succored the needs   of the living
and dead   Today   for different reasons
the vaccine   offers no guarantee
against the limits of reason

Circle

to make words not
diverse from the facts
is how the shadows cast
earthly deeds into eternal
afterlight, *stil novo* miracle
whip, this poor. old. tired. horse
Astolfo rides to the Moone
a carafe all voyde of spot
finds in the valley of things lost
the difference spreading wit
to make words not

Athos

All those monks on Athos
dotting the rugged Peninsula
upkeeping monasteries on ridges
deep in the folds, along winding
cobbled paths, deep in the woods,
they sleep for three hours,
rise into prayer, each chore
a prayer, pure divine act, pilgrims
blessed, ferry from Ouranoupolis
to kiss the priest's hand

Meals of fruits and vegetables, grains
and fish, I see them onscreen
working in the orchards, the fields
in prayer, painting and engineering
in prayer, archiving and sewing

In quiet contemplation, centuries
before and after, pass into ever after

All their skills brought to the table
Beards flowing in the ritual air
Waiting list for residence long

Walk to the iron cross by the sea
A hand raises the rite of centuries

Sacred garden, bleeding icon,
song sung by the grace of the One

sovereign, the state their land
kept free of women and children
under the eye of the Virgin Mary

Three Notes on Translation

1.

December 21, 1853, Emily Dickinson to Emily Ford:
"Dear Emily, when it came, and hidden by your veil you
stood before us all and made those promises, and when we
kissed you, all, and went back to our homes, it seemed to me
translation, not any earthly thing, and if a little after you'd
ridden on the wind, it would not have surprised me."

2.

Philip Dick in *The Three Stigmata of Palmer Eldritch*:
"He himself was a believer; he affirmed the miracle of translation—
the near-sacred moment in which the miniature artifacts of the layout
no longer merely represented Earth but *became* Earth."

3.

Li Rongxi translates Tripitaka-Master Xuanzang's *Notes
on the Western Lands*, as recorded and edited by Sramana Bianji:[*]
"Excessive embellishments would render a translation too
flowery in style, but if it is too simple it would be inelegant.
Only when it is done in a plain style without ornamentation
and written elegantly without being dull can a work be free
of grave blunders and be accepted as a good translation. Laozi says,
'Florid sayings are not trustworthy, and trustworthy words are not florid.'"

---

[*] The monk Bianji had an affair with Emperor Taizong's daughter, Princess Gaoyang. For this, he was cut in
half at the waist.

Travel Writing

The ancients called it "jade
column," doctors "ancestral tendon,"
commonly known as "feminine stem"
or "male tool," "little brother," "turtle head,"
"meat stick," "turtle dove," "doohickey,"
Children say "little chicken"
unaware it could one day lead
to "the garden of peach blossoms"

■

In the Book of Last Words
the Old Master says,
"Your life is not your own."
「為人子者毋以有己，
為人臣者毋以有己」

■

In the Book of Last Words
Kumarajiva says to the sangha, "If you turn
to the meaning of the sutras I've translated,
you will find no errors nor omissions. You
will know this is true when you burn
my body and my tongue remains whole."*

---

* Indeed, Kumarajiva's tongue remained intact and didn't burn. See the *Gaoseng Zhuan* (高僧传, Lives of
Eminent Monks), compiled around 530 AD by the monk Huijiao.

Mencius

On a mission with no position
the ideal of state as benevolent
government, that those most skilled
in war should suffer the most
severe punishment, knowing what
proceeds from you will assuredly
return, in the practice of benevolence,
for "benevolence" gloss "human"
the two conjoined making "the way,"
nurture your inner nature of rightness
and retain your true heart, if gone astray,
can still be sought, the sole aim of learning
is to strive after this strayed heart, clear
the heart of grass and continue along
the mountain pass, to look within
yourself when you fail to achieve
your purpose, trace the lines and
wait patiently to meet the poet's
purpose, with sympathetic
understanding listen to the heart's
music, its onward flowing thoughts will
attain new depths of meaning,
unfolding the context through natural
ties, nurturing a compassion of
benevolence, like things cut, then filed,
like things carved, then polished

Kuafu

"It was not only Kuafu who had the strength to
chase the sun to the remotest realms."
—Sramana Bianji, 646 CE

On a run
          straight out to sun
                    Kuafu chases the light
     on Mt. Carry-the-Sky
crosses Yu valley north
          drinks the rivers and lakes
                    Along the way
     I follow the lines
made of dust and thirst
          ahead and behind, ties
                    packed with broken
          stones, track gauge ballast
bearing the wheel load, steel
          strips welded and fixed
                    ribbonrails
          at the gateless crossing
Ocotillo tongues
          ablaze at the stem-tips
                    jackrabbit's zigzag
          song
of the hermit thrush
          rises out of the brush
                    open breeze picks up
          grass tassel seeds
Body's breath
          measures water
                    sweet life-giving
          breath quickens, sweat, air-
cooled skin
          blood pulse water-
                    flow waves
          cycle loss, trails

of salt, igneous
    aquifer under-
        ground layers
    seep up in the dark
resonant depths
    we start awake
        with a cry of recognition
    surfaces to sun
Molecules dance
    against the last
        cadence, train
    steady trestle
loose spikes
    mouth dries
        eyes tear behind
    shades, pace
wanes past
    the divided grave
        Lines run
    after sun
Kuafu chases the light
    to the remotest realms
        no sum of water
    can quench his thirst
what inner dragon
    no god could overcome
        He dies
    on the track, staff
roots into earth
    grows into Peach Tree
        Forest, dragon
    flies off
for the southern lands
    Rains follow

In the Book of Last Words
Joseph M. W. Turner says,
"The sun is God."

In the Book of Last Words
Eddie Johnson says before his execution,
"Goodbye, sun, I love you."

In the Book of Last Words
Qiu Miaojin has written another
book *loyal to an everlasting love*.
「忠於一椿永恆之愛」

Hey, Marfa
grant us the grace
of a certain candor
and the *firm perswasion*
to vow for more
than what is offered
by the news
each day
Each
winged seed sown
in your dirt
rain
drops water
polyps
pop out, branch
ing into sun
desert coral

"These snowy streets dammit motherfucker go fuck yourself"
—Watanabe Hakusen, 1937 (translated by Hiroaki Sato)

Snow
more snow in our hearts
reams of snow spin down from on high
down the pressure gradients
and icy rimes
down the acid troposphere
man-made with time
down the windows and sails, mountains and pines
down the bridges, poles, rays, wires, waves, arrows, rails
down the streetlamps and stuttering wings
down the locker rooms, seats, signs, and screens, down the ballots and cliffs
down the stations, stacks, scarves, bells, plants, monuments, towers, tombs, eves snow
pours out of the breathless deceptions
the deceptive aggressions, the rich
currencies mired with means, snow
pours into the leaves and ravines, the forgotten
caves, cracked cisterns, ruptured vessels, snow,
more snow
whirls down the updrafts
blows into squares, blankets the slides,
seesaw, merry-go-round, phrases
float round and round
the covered ground
like a silent adagio, like fractured ice floes
winds of snow unravel the mind
pass through the barrier, fill the folds
and crevices, turn shapes into shapelessness,
more and more snow
heaps onto branches, weighted
evergreens droop and bend
snow gusts swirl down the dome
stolen sky oval clouds

thick iron-gray depthless mists
edgeless beyond
the snow rushing in
blinding the sun, endless
snow
relentless drifts
bury the grasses
fatten the snowfields
merge into snowbanks, flakes
fall like broken words, like notes
torn from a score, walls and walls
of snow shadows cross to and fro
causes known and unknown, no
refuge from the snow, no face
clear in the air, the storm's
flurry . . . that holds us, plays
with us and discards us
light lies, thirst
grows, *eyes scan the heavens*
mind cleaves to earth
snow piles snow
snow
snow
snow
snow
clouds break, snow
still snows, fast then slow,
melts or sublimates
blurs, returns
summer fall
snow
more snow in our hearts

What is

or is true as
Happiness

Birth
A pure river

Conditions for the equal good
to be as wise and fortunate

at the start

Lost in the pursuit

Under a white oak
two children sitting back
to back on a plank swing, calling

The hand
that touches the earth
to witness

Presses the metal latch, opens
the screen door out from home

sunlight, pond water silence
damselfly at rest on a frond

Having come with you
this far into the drafty air

In the Book of Last Words
Ed Dorn says, "Once the poem is thought
it returns home to its own fire."

◾

In the Book of Last Words
John Burroughs says on a train out West,
"How far are we from home?"

◾

In the Book of Last Words
Gerard Manley Hopkins says,
"I am so happy … I am so happy."

Paris 1777, Rousseau on a walk:
"Is the moment when we have to die
the time to learn how we should have lived?"

■

New York City, circa 1933,
Fairfield Porter on a walk
after his anatomy and dissection
drawing class: "People
look so beautiful
just because they are alive."

■

Marfa, October 9, 1999, Rackstraw
quotes Henry James in his Chinati talk:
"'Really, universally, relations stop nowhere,
and the exquisite problem of the artist is eternally
but to draw, by a geometry of his own,
the circle in which they shall happily
appear to do so.'"

Circle

outside of Turfan
in front of a tomb built for Muslims
out of air-dried bricks
enclosed by graduated battlements
at the junction
where the wall meets the structure
of the center dome
leans a Buddhist Wheel
on the desert sands
outside of Turfan

Cave

I entered the cave by way of Ellora
others have known as Aladra, or Alura,
its level hill signals
no human activity inside it
outside its gardens of luxuriant vegetation
and abundance of water, the falls
tumble down like a reincarnated god
dancing down the crystal threads
down the blue cliff face
faces forgotten faces fixed
you who shaped the mandala streams
while awake in a dream, the three-tiered halls
from darkness to light, shrines
leap out of the walls, carved
bodhisattvas, for two centuries, centuries
before, your hands materialized the mudras in stone,
visualized the pradakshina past
the pillars and pilasters, the ritual cisterns,
open book on a lotus, sketches of forms
untying the knots, a single step
completes the design, I had chosen
the unexamined life and failed, my failings
haunting me here, this place your reverence
named, your names concealed in its signs
triple-bud stem, raised diamond thunderbolt,
garland and song, I was drawn
to the uppermost articulation
in my circumambulations, fine dust
caught in the sunlight, in the gaze
of the stalking lions, against the darkest
recesses, the Perfected One's summoning gesture
for your heroic deeds asked no remembrance
in the image the silence, I was drawn
to the doorway where Janguli sits with royal ease

I performed the sacred rite
as it had been handed down through me
my feet blackened with earth
and in her cognizance she clarified
the poison surging within me

■

In the Book of Last Words
Bashō says through Hiro,
"Falling ill on a journey my dreams run round a withered field."

Wisteria Youth Mirror

Clarity in no-clarity
Feeling in no-feeling
Appearance detached from appearance
as if holding out a spray of flowers
where the "flower" is the performing body
the heart the form beneath the mask

In the Book of Last Words
Vicente Huidobro asks
for a mirror

"Life

is an affair of places,"
for Stevens in "Adagia"
as for Monk Nōin of the late Heian
who notes the village cove of Akashi
on the Inland Sea among the *uta-makura,*
place names to be sung (see Sato's
Snow in a Silver Bowl), Kakinomoto no
Hitomaro's morning mist   growing
light slow   the bay   lone   boat
fades   as it lightens   toward
a desert   island   I think on,   - a - - a

Woods

At home in woods
we wander well-
marked trails
yellow   red   blue
sole diversions off-
trail: little
son little daughter
looking for mushrooms

Substation

"This wire is my redeemer."
—H. D. Thoreau

Conducting lines golden in the light

Waves illuminate the sun's last words
on the morning faces, rippling turtleback
slope, lone cypress, lone elm, poles

greet a few low-pitched roofs at the end
of the road, pink posts planted in a row small
heaps of dirt, weed clumps, square shadow door-

way cast on a wall, zigzag edge veers round
the posts, runs the fence perimeter, divides
the vicinity from the mind's machinery

swerves magnetic for the H-frame gnomon
Dawn tracks, empty block, rolling sphere lightning
rods, tiny brushstrokes against the surging storm

Spirit living energy, the matter—*not with the fire
in me now*—of survival, where the windswept sands
fade to asphalt, and the lines like the strings of a lyre

strung through the sky, converge on a visible
chord sustained across the urban wilderness

Slow desert sustenance, evidence of the true

reflection in the inner light outside the picture

I, interloper,
who dares to add
these grains to the sands

what do you know
of yes and no
of wind and bone
of dust and thirst
of the ever-shifting rose
in the ferriferous
radiant record of the real
sung from the well
aligned in the heliosphere
can you make the air
tremble with brightness
draw the form from the ash
sinter hope's filaments
with your unsung song
hear the moon's echo
submerged in the mirror
your uncertain manifoldness
your sleep I sail

List of Paintings and Drawings by Rackstraw Downes

All images courtesy of the Betty Cuningham Gallery; photographs of the drawings by Paul Brodeur. With thanks to the Lannan Foundation for permission to use the images of the paintings and to the Betty Cuningham Gallery for permission to use the images of the drawings.

Paintings

5   *From Marfa to Presidio Via the Grid, 2003–2004 Part 1—Alamito Creek Substation, Marfa.* 13½ x 34½ inches. Oil on canvas. Lannan Collection.

37   *From Marfa to Presidio Via the Grid, 2003–2004 Part 2—Downtown Marfa Substation.* 13½ x 30¾ inches. Oil on canvas. Lannan Collection.

76–77   *From Marfa to Presidio Via the Grid, 2003–2004 Part 3—On a Ranch Between Marfa and Shafter, with the Cienega and Bryant Ranch Substations in the Distance.* 13½ x 46⅞ inches. Oil on canvas. Lannan Collection.

109   *From Marfa to Presidio Via the Grid, 2003–2004 Part 4—Substation on a Ridge in the Shafter Mountain.* 13½ x 19⅜ inches. Oil on canvas. Lannan Collection.

143   *From Marfa to Presidio Via the Grid, 2003–2004 Part 5—Presidio Substation, the Sierra de la Santa Cruz in the Distance.* 13½ x 37¼ inches. Oil on canvas. Lannan Collection.

Drawings

57   *Alamito Creek Substation, Marfa,* March 2003. 19 x 28½ inches. Graphite on paper.
Alamito Creek Substation, Marfa, March 2003. 12 x 27 inches. Graphite on paper.

58   *Downtown Marfa Substation, Looking East,* March 2003. 6¼ x 18½ inches. Graphite on paper.
Downtown Marfa Substation, March 2003. 9⅜ x 29½ inches. Graphite on paper.
Downtown Marfa Substation, Looking East, March 2003. 13 x 32¼ inches. Graphite on paper.

59   *Downtown Marfa Substation,* March 2003. 13 x 35 inches. Graphite on paper.
Bryant Substation on the Shurley Ranch with Cienega Substation in the Distance, 2003. 11 x 40 inches. Graphite on paper.
Bryant Substation on the Shurley Ranch with Cienega Substation in the Distance, 2003. 12¼ x 30¾ inches. Graphite on paper.

60   *Two Small Transformers on the Shurley Ranch,* March 2003. 11 x 31 inches. Graphite on paper.
Substation in the Shafter Mountains, Looking West, 2004. 13⁹⁄₁₆ x 34½ inches. Graphite on paper.

61   *Substation in the Shafter Mountains, Looking West,* 2004. 9½ x 33 inches. Graphite on paper.
Substation in the Mountains at Shafter, 2004. (text on front) 1:30 pm light midday on mountain. 9½ x 25 inches. Graphite on paper.

62   *Substation, Presidio, March 2003.* 13¹⁄₂₆ x 34⅞ inches. Graphite on paper.

Index

Titles in italic. First lines of untitled poems in roman.

Jeffrey Yang is the author of the poetry collections *Vanishing-Line* and *An Aquarium* (Winner of the PEN/Joyce Osterweil Award). He is the translator of Nobel Peace Prize Laureate Liu Xiaobo's *June Fourth Elegies*, Bei Dao's *City Gate, Open Up*, and Ahtmajan Osman's *Uyghurland, the Farthest Exile*, and is the editor of the poetry anthologies *Birds, Beasts, and Seas* and *Time of Grief*, as well as a volume of Walt Whitman's poetry and prose, *The Sea Is a Continual Miracle*. Yang was born in Escondido, CA, and has lived in Edinburgh (Scotland), Lianyungang (China), and Berlin (Germany), where he was a 2017–2018 DAAD artist-in-residence. He works as an editor for New Directions and New York Review Books, and lives in Beacon, NY.

Rackstraw Downes is a painter, teacher, and essayist. His books include *Nature and Art Are Physical, In Relation to the Whole, Under the Gowanus and Razor-Wire Journal*, as well as an edited volume of Fairfield Porter's criticism, *Art in Its Own Terms*. His work is in the permanent collections of The Art Institute of Chicago, The Museum of Modern Art, The Metropolitan Museum of Art, The Whitney Museum of American Art, and the National Gallery of Art, among other collections. Downes is represented by Betty Cuningham Gallery, New York. He lives between New York, NY and Presidio, TX.

The text of *Hey, Marfa* is set in Arno Pro.
Book design by Rachel Holscher.
Composition by Bookmobile Design and Digital
Publisher Services, Minneapolis, Minnesota.
Manufactured by Versa Press on acid-free paper.